## The stories at this level

These stories are fuller and a little more
They introduce a greater number of ch
of West Street. The words are repeated
are longer. At this level you should beg... ..... ...........
independent reading more.

Before you start reading with your children, read the story and activities
first yourself, so that you become familiar with the text and the best way to
give it expression and emphasis when reading it aloud.

Always sit comfortably with your child, so that both of you can see the
book easily.

Read the story to your child, making it sound as interesting as possible.
Add comments on the story and the pictures if you wish. Encourage your
child to participate actively in the reading, to turn over the pages, and to
become involved in the story and characters.

This may be enough for one sitting, but don't give your child the idea that
the book is finished with. Encourage your child to take the book away and
to look through it alone.

Next time you look at the book with your child, suggest "Let's read the
story together. You join in with me." The text in the speech bubbles is often
the same as the text at the bottom of the page, so one of you can read the
text in the bubbles, and one can read the text at the bottom of the page.
This time encourage your child to guess words from the context.
Follow the words with your finger under them as you read. Don't stop
to repeat words; keep the interest up and the story line flowing along.

Now ask your child, "Do you want to read the story to me this time?"
If your child would like to do this, join in where necessary if help is needed.

## The activities at this level

The activities at the back of the book need not be completed at once.
They are not a test, but will help your child to remember the words and

stories and to develop further the skills required for becoming a fluent reader.

The activities are often divided into three parts.

One part is designed to encourage you both to talk about the stories, and to link them where possible with your child's own experiences. Encourage your child to predict what will happen and to recall the main events of the story. Change the wording of the story as much as you like and encourage your children to tell you about the story in their own way.

One part encourages children to look back through the book to find general or specific things in the text or the pictures. Your child learns to begin to look at the text itself, and to recognise individual words and letters more precisely. The activities state clearly when you should give a letter its name, and when you should sound it out. The activities also introduce more writing, largely copying from words in the original story. If your children find this too difficult, copy the words onto a piece of paper for them to trace over.

One part suggests drawing or writing activities which will help your children feel they are contributing actively to the story in the book.

When you and your child have finished all the activities, read the story together again before you move on to another book. Your child should now feel secure with it and enjoy being able to read the story to you.

**BEFORE READING THE STORY.** Turn to page 28 and do the first activity with your child.

# Dressing up

by Helen Arnold

Illustrated by Tony Kenyon

A Piccolo Original
In association with Macmillan Education

Hello, Tamla.
Hello, Liz.

What shall we play, Tamla?
Let's play dressing up.

Come up, Liz.

We can find some dressing up things in here. Mum won't mind.

Look at this lovely hat.

I've got a hat too.

Look at my shoes.

I've got some shoes too.

I've got a pretty dress too.

I've got a pretty dress too.

Look at these lovely beads.

Look at these lovely beads.

Look at these pretty ear-rings.

I like dressing up.

I like dressing up too.

You look like a princess.

And you look like my Mum.

I'm Princess Tamla.

And who is Liz?

Liz is you, Mum!

# Things to talk about with your children

**1.** Let's look at the cover of the book before we read it.

What do you think the story is going to be about?
What's going to happen?

**2.** Whose clothes were Tamla and Liz trying on?

Why did Tamla look like a princess?
Why did Liz look like Tamla's Mum?
Did Mrs Singh mind them dressing up? How do you know?

**3.** Let's find page 5 in the book. I'm going to tell you something that happens there. It might be true or it might not be true. You tell me which.

Is it true that it was Tamla who thought of dressing up?
Is it true that Liz tried the ear-rings on?

Now let's find page 24.

Is it true that Liz said she was a princess?

# Things for your child to do

**1.** Make four cards. Write one of these words on each card.

# hat shoes dress beads

Spread the cards out and ask your child:

Can you point to the word that says what you wear on your feet?

Now point to the card that says what you wear round your neck.

Now point to the word that says what you put on your body.

Now point to the word that says what you wear on your head.

Let your child draw each of the items and then either place the words under the appropriate drawings or copy the words.

**2.** What did Tamla wear and what did Liz wear? Make a list, with your child drawing the items and you writing the words under each drawing.

| These activities and skills: | will help your children to: |
|---|---|
| Looking and remembering | hold a story in their heads, retell it in their own words. |
| Listening, being able to tell the difference between sounds | remember sounds in words and link spoken words with the words they see in print. |
| Naming things and using different words to explain or retell events | recognise different words in print, build their vocabulary and guess at the meaning of words. |
| Matching, seeing patterns, similarities and differences | recognise letters, see patterns within words, use the patterns to read 'new' words and split long words into syllables. |
| Knowing the grammatical patterns of spoken language | guess the word-order in reading. |
| Anticipating what is likely to happen next in a story | guess what the next sentence or event is likely to be about. |
| Colouring, getting control of pencils and pens, copying and spelling | produce their own writing, which will help them to understand the way English is written. |
| Understanding new experiences by linking them to what they already know | read with understanding and think about what they have read. |
| Understanding their own feelings and those of others | enjoy and respond to stories and identify with the characters. |

First published 1988 by Pan Books Ltd,
Cavaye Place, London SW10 9PG

9 8 7 6 5 4 3 2 1

Editorial consultant: Donna Bailey

© Pan Books Ltd and Macmillan Publishers Ltd 1988. Text © Helen Arnold 1988

British Library Cataloguing in Publication Data
Arnold, Helen
Dressing up. — (Read together Level 2).
I. Title  II. Series
428.6         PR6051.R61/
ISBN 0–330–30215–9

Printed in Hong Kong

This book is sold subject to the condition that it shall not, by way of trade or otherwise be lent, re-sold, hired out or otherwise circulated without the publisher's prior consent in any form of binding or cover other than that in which it is published and without a similar condition including this condition being imposed on the subsequent purchaser

Whilst the advice and information in this book are believed to be true and accurate at the time of going to press, neither the author nor the publisher can accept any legal responsibility or liability for any errors or omissions that may be made